CÉZANNE

Cézanne

Text and Notes by

KEITH ROBERTS

TUDOR PUBLISHING COMPANY
New York

TUDOR PUBLISHING COMPANY

New York, 1967

Library of Congress Catalog Card Number: 67–19840

Printed in Japan

CÉZANNE, THE CLASSICAL IMPRESSIONIST

Of all the great painters that France produced in the 19th century, none is so revered at the present time as Paul Cézanne. His pictures are admired alike by artists and critics, and by collectors, whose competitive enthusiasm has insured that the painter, who for years had the greatest difficulty in selling his works, has become the most expensive of all 19th- and 20th-century masters. The intensity of this admiration is due to a number of factors; first and foremost, the intrinsic quality of Cézanne's art, but also to the very evident relationship between his painting and subsequent developments in both American and European art.

In its simplifications and passive monumentality, the treatment of the human form in the late Bathers series (Plate 87) anticipates the early Cubist pictures of Picasso and Braque, while passages in all the later works, a piece of drapery, perhaps, or the sleeve of a coat, have the flat, two-dimensional character of abstract painting. A fine Cézanne is thus doubly precious. Lawrence Gowing, an English critic and painter, much influenced in his own work by Cézanne, expressed the point well when he wrote in 1953 that "For us Cézanne is a touchstone. He is like a patron saint. Whoever does not feel the force of his art and the heroic virtue of his example, whoever (we might say) can name easily a greater painter, is not only not of his time—more, is not on the threshold of valuing what it is that is precious to this century."

Paul Cézanne was born in Aix, in Provence, in 1839. Like Degas, he was the son of a banker who did not at all approve of an artistic career. And like Degas, he briefly studied law. But even though he was often assailed by doubts, and at one point

*Early
years*

actually gave up art for banking, Cézanne was determined to become a painter. He was aided and abetted by Émile Zola, who had been a close friend since childhood. They grew up together, read the same books (especially the Romantic poets Hugo and Musset), wrote, and confided in each other, as adolescents do. When Zola left for Paris in 1858, they exchanged letters regularly. This friendship, which held firm until 1886, was perhaps the most profound relationship that Cézanne ever had.

It was Zola's encouragement that was instrumental in persuading Cézanne to come to Paris in 1861. In the capital he met Camille Pissarro, the great Impressionist painter, at the Atelier Suisse; but he felt discouraged and returned to Aix. After a few months, and with that abruptness that was always discernible in his behavior, Cézanne rejoined Zola in Paris, where he remained, with intermittent visits to Aix, until 1870. His life was never particularly eventful and, again like Degas, he always had sufficient means to support him through the years of critical and public hostility. He married, but this was not a great success—though he idolized his son—and in later years he became more and more of a recluse. One thing, and one thing only mattered: painting.

Cézanne was always diffident about his own work, and it was only in his very last years that he would allow himself to express to friends a certain measure of satisfaction with what he was doing. Highly intelligent, neurotic and morose, he was the least complacent of artists. But then in his youth he would have had few reasons for self-satisfaction. No other painter of comparable stature began as unpromisingly. Early pictures like *The Orgy* (Pl. 3) or *The Picnic* (Pl. 4) are clumsy, ill-drawn and badly designed. They are as ugly as some of Rembrandt's early paintings, but without the saving grace of the great Dutch master's prodigious technique.

The truth of the matter is that Cézanne had no facility. Eventual mastery was acquired painfully and laboriously. The ineptness of these early works—"early" rather than "youthful" since some of them were produced when Cézanne was in his late twenties—should not, however, be allowed to blind one to the presence of several characteristics that are an indispensable part of all his finest work. Partly what makes so many of the early paintings uncomfortable to look at is the hardly disguised intensity of feeling. This was a direct expression of Cézanne's own passionate nature, and while it is a source of embarrassment in the early work, it is precisely what gives to his mature and considered paintings, with their complex trellis-work of strokes, an underlying warmth and power. Equally important for his subsequent development was Cézanne's directness of attack. Uncle Dominic (Pl. 1) and his father (Pl. 2) are presented foursquare on the canvas, without finesse. The thick paint is applied partly with a knife, imparting to the surface the uneven, tactile character of a sculpted relief, and it is used with a heavy insistence, as though Cézanne would assert and try to prove that he could conjure up presences on canvas by sheer force.

In the beginning, Cézanne's desire to express passionate feeling led him to emulate the robust art of painters such as Courbet and Delacroix. Courbet influenced his dark color scale and impasted technique, while it was to Delacroix that he mainly owed the strong color harmonies and sinuous composition of *The Orgy*. The disadvantage, as a formative influence, of Delacroix and Courbet, and of Manet (see Pls. 4 and 8), lay in the sheer sophistication of their art. It was therefore extremely fortunate that Cézanne—who in spite of the early fantasies was committed to depicting modern life—should have come under the influence of Camille Pissarro.

They worked together in the period 1872–4 and Cézanne always recognized that it had been Pissarro, the "humble and colossal Pissarro," who had really shown him the way. Pissarro was an Impressionist, that is to say, he was concerned with recording optical impressions and noting how they were modified by distance and the play of light; but at the same time he did not al-

7

low himself to forget the example and teaching of Corot, a staunch upholder of a classical tradition of landscape going back to the great 17th-century masters Claude and Poussin. Without sacrificing any immediacy of effect, Pissarro was thus able to impart to his landscapes a stability of design not always found in the work of Monet, Renoir and other contemporaries.

Pissarro

Pissarro's particular form of Impressionism attracted Cézanne for three main reasons. It offered him an objective form of subject matter, something concrete in place of his vague longings. The technique itself was more amenable to examination and emulation than the prodigious stylistic feats of Delacroix. Finally, Pissarro's carefully constructed compositions appealed to Cézanne's own latent classical tendencies, that desire for artistic order that was to become the mainspring of his art.

La Maison du Pendu (Pl. 9) is an excellent example of Cézanne's style at its closest to Pissarro. There is the same kind of firm composition, with the vertical element emphasized by the trees and the edge of the house; the same light tonality—so different from the early canvases—and the same use of the brush stroke, now small and dabbed on rather than drawn across the canvas, to convey local color and suggest structure.

Reality and illusion

The main difference between the two artists, and it is a crucial one, lay in their attitude to illusionism. Cézanne's painting is far less atmospheric than a Pissarro. The effect of sunlight and distance is implied, certainly, but unstressed; just as in the portraits (Pls. 14, 16, 17, 26, 27) there is little or no attempt to differentiate between the textures of hair and skin. Lack of facility made it extremely hard for Cézanne to accomplish what an average Salon painter took in his stride. By a largely subconscious process, familiar to most of us, Cézanne came to disregard situations in which he knew instinctively he could not succeed. This rejection of a conventional standard of illusionism released him from the tyranny of strict representation and allowed him to re-create form according to his own standards.

Painters who have no problems are seldom aware that there are problems. Cézanne, by nature shy and diffident, was acutely conscious of his own shortcomings. But far from being a fatal encumbrance, this deficiency slowed up, as it were, the whole process of painting, and made a naturally introspective man constantly reflect on the nature of art. In the process, ironically enough, Cézanne evolved one of the most ambitious styles in the history of Western art; ambitious not in the sense that he wanted to work on a large scale (most of his paintings are small) or illustrate lofty themes, but in the extremely complex relationship he wanted to establish between reality and pictorial illusion. Few artists have ever made so many demands of a single brush stroke.

These more complex aims are already apparent in the work that Cézanne produced in the second half of the 1870s, and particularly in some of the portraits, such as those of Madame Cézanne (Pl. 16) and Victor Chocquet (Pl. 17). Madame Cézanne is seated in an armchair, her hands clasped in her lap. The pose is uncompromisingly frontal, as is the upper half of the figure of Chocquet. Logically, Chocquet's legs, as well as the chair he is sitting in, are at a three-quarter angle, but the forms give the impression of being in profile. In both portraits we are aware of the solidity of the figure—Madame Cézanne is as immovable as an enthroned ruler—and also that the figure is painted.

It is obvious that the painter wished to create some kind of illusion of form and to persuade the spectator that he was looking at figures sitting in rooms, but it is also clear that he did not wish to conceal, in any part of a picture, the fact that it *is* an illusion. For the art that conceals art one might say that Cézanne substituted the art that creates art. That is partly why one is so acutely aware of the physical surface of a Cézanne picture. Rich and emphatic texture is a common-place in the history of European painting, but before Cézanne it had usually been an adjunct of decoration, almost like a cadenza in a concerto, or with artists such as Rembrandt and Titian the by-product of a very broad

9

technique. Cézanne made it the token of a philosophy.

Yet the often awkward, primitive, earthy character of his figures—there are even moments when one feels that the beautiful *Portrait of a Peasant* (Pl. 77) might have been painted by a peasant—should never be allowed to conceal the essentially intellectual nature of Cézanne's art. He was an "intellectual painter," just as Henry James was an "intellectual novelist." In both cases want of facility (James lacked empathy, the ability to get inside a character completely, as Tolstoy or Flaubert could) led to a concentration on analytical art. Gustave Geffroy (Pl. 72) is a powerful presence on the canvas, but the sheer process of conjuring up, stroke by laborious stroke, the weighty, almost monolithic body, and organizing the forms into a design of classical inevitability, has robbed the painting of a certain spontaneous vitality. The picture is very grand and immensely subtle, as well as being very delicately executed, but it is also a little remote; just as many of James's fictional characters are endowed with substance and significance and yet are curiously lacking in immediacy. But then both Cézanne and James were too aware of the barrier between art and life for life, or at least a direct sense of life, to pass easily into their work. They were perhaps too conscious of what James, in his art criticism, was wont to, call the "plastic obligation."

Cézanne's visual analysis was extremely complex because he felt that there were a great many pictorial issues to be reconciled. And the single stroke of paint had to bear the brunt of his intentions. He was suspicious of line and outline, in fact, of all the implications of the classical method of drawing. "Pure drawing," he once said, "is an abstraction." Drawing and outline were not distinct since everything in nature had color. He told Émile Bernard that "while one paints, one draws; the more the color harmonizes, the more precise becomes the drawing. When the color is rich, the form is at its height. The contrasts and relations of tone comprise the secret of drawing and form."

Cézanne's contention is borne out by an examination of almost any one of his mature pictures. It is particularly clear in the still-lifes such as those reproduced in Pls. 24 and 25. Cézanne felt that every form—an apple, a head, a rock, a crumpled napkin, etc.— could be reduced, pictorially, to a number of facets, for each of which there was an equivalent stroke of paint. Each form, too, had a certain color or mixture of colors, and the three-dimensional appearance of an object was established visually by the changes in the color or tone caused by the play of light. Cézanne was true to the Impressionist doctrine in paying great attention to light. Each stroke of paint, therefore, had both to express the color of objects and the way it was affected by light and shadow, and it also had to define changes of direction in the modelling that would create an impression of solidity. The green apples in Pl. 24 show this process at its simplest. Where the light falls directly, the surface is pale green, but as the fruit curves away into shadow the green tones become progressively darker. And as the tones of green deepen, they show not only how the light alters but also how the surface of the apple recedes from the eye. "The main thing," as Cézanne once remarked, "is the modelling; one shouldn't even say modelling, but modulating." This process demanded the most delicate perceptions and intense concentration. It is no wonder that Cézanne would gaze at objects for hours and pause for ten minutes at a time before applying one more small stroke to his canvas.

Form and color

"The main thing is the modelling"

Cézanne also came to believe that the same stroke of paint should contribute to the underlying structure of the painting. Once again like James, Cézanne was fascinated by the problem of structure, and he recognized that the real weakness of Impressionism was that its very stress on the impression, and what was fleeting, would lead to triviality. He once said that he wanted to make of Impressionism something solid and durable, like the art of the museums. Cézanne's pictorial solution to the problem was to emphasize a geometric stability of design. The tables in the still-

11

lifes (Pls. 24, 25, 43, 48, 63) are invariably set down on the canvas four-square, their edges parallel with the bottom or sides of the painting. Furniture and wallpaper, or the panels of doors (Pls. 17, 27, 47, 48, 76) are also made to yield up a reassuring geometrical emphasis. It is hardly surprising that Cézanne should have stressed the virtues of the circle, the cylinder and the cone, even if speaking in a limited context.

Once he had mastered this method of composition in the 1880s, Cézanne was able to introduce into his work all kinds of asymmetry, as well as complex curves, without destroying the equilibrium of his designs. With its clusters of ripe, round fruit and mountainous cloth, the great Louvre *Still-Life* (Pl. 83) makes something of the same sensuous impression as *The Orgy*. A richness has been retained, but it has acquired greater power through being subjected to an intense classical discipline.

This feeling for structure was not confined to the design. The precise way the paint strokes were applied was equally important, and in the works of his early maturity—such as the *Still-Life* on Pl. 24—he would often lay all the strokes on in the same overall direction. Experience allowed him to vary his touch, though it always remained precisely that: the stroke of paint, in some of the later pictures separated even by tiny areas of white canvas. It is this constant emphasis on the strokes set down side by side, one after another, which contributes so much to the relentless character of Cézanne's paintings. There is no sudden swoop on the objective, no wild dash for victory expressed in long, spontaneous strokes of the brush, but a steady, even progression; just as in James's novels we move, sentence by stately sentence, towards the culmination of a Grand Design.

Such a degree of control is admirable; and generally speaking, it can be said to yield the most satisfactory results in an artist's middle period when technique and observation are in balance. But with the passing of the years, as the freshness of response wains, stylistic disciplines are apt to take charge. And certainly in many of his later paintings, Cézanne was inclined, like James in his last novels, to substitute the method for the subject. Some of the late landscapes, particularly the views of the Montagne Sainte-Victoire, can be tedious to look at; and in spite of the fact that he labored over them for years, Cézanne could really make very little out of the series of Bathers (Pl. 87). What redeems them is his unfailing sense of color.

The strongly conceptual element in Cézanne's art, the way it can be taken to pieces and examined, stroke by stroke, is a symptom of his essential classicism. This has had some unfortunate consequences for which the artist was not responsible. Cézanne suffered the fate reserved for influential classicists since the Renaissance, and one that had already overcome Raphael, Poussin and Ingres. His work became a pictorial text book; and with certain important exceptions—Picasso, Braque and Matisse among them—the influence was disastrous. Dozens of painters, often too obscure even to be forgotten, modelled themselves on his example without realizing the extent to which Cézanne's art represented a complex and unrepeatable fusion of passion, intellect, nerves, experiment, observation and sensitivity.

*Influ-
ence of
Cézanne*

What his academic followers, too, often overlooked was that Cézanne belonged to the generation of the Impressionists; he had all their faith in a form of art rooted in the direct observation of everyday life. When he made his famous, oft-quoted remark that he wanted "to do Poussin over again, from nature," he was expressing, with some precision, his central aim: the reconciliation of ordered pictorial form with a strict record of natural appearance. Cézanne is the only great artist to have succeeded equally in portraiture, landscape and still-life, partly because he brought to bear on the rocky countryside of his native Provence, the faces of his patient sitters, and the fruit he set out on the table, the same passionate scrutiny.

*The
Impres-
sionist
aspect*

What sets the final seal of greatness upon Cézanne's work is this element of observation and of what it permits, the entry into

an extra-ordinary world of considered forms of what is ordinary
and unconsidered—the peasant in his shabby clothes, the men in
the bistro playing cards, the trees by a garden wall, a vase of
flowers, bottles, the rumpled table cloth. It is perhaps his most
remarkable achievement that he should have succeeded in enno-
bling them without ever losing or concealing their perfectly ordinary character. Cézanne was one of the very few artists of the 19th
century to ignore the superficial apparatus of the classical style,
the myths and temples and togas, while retaining its underlying
disciplines. As early as 1877, a perceptive critic wrote what might
almost stand for the painter's epitaph: "M. Cézanne is in his
work a Greek of the great period; his canvases have the calm
and heroic serenity of the paintings and terra-cottas of antiquity. . . ."

KEITH ROBERTS

14

RECOMMENDED READING

Rewald, J., ed.: *Paul Cézanne: Letters*. London, 1941.

Fry, Roger: *Cézanne, A Study of His Development*. London, 1927. (Second Edition, London, 1952.)

Schapiro, Meyer: *Cézanne*. New York, 1952.

Mack, Gerstle: *The Life of Paul Cézanne*. London, 1935.

Venturi, Lionello: *Cézanne, son art—son oeuvre*. 2 vols., Paris, 1936. (Indispensable for any study of Cézanne. A revised and enlarged edition is in preparation.)

Novotny, F.: *Cézanne.* London, 1961.

PAUL CÉZANNE

1839   January 19th, born at Aix-en-Provence. Forebears are artisans and small tradesmen of Piedmontese origin. His father, a former hatter, has prospered, and is manager of a bank.

1852–8   Student at the Collège Bourbon at Aix. Begins close friendship with fellow student Émile Zola, which will last until 1886. With Baille and Numa Coste they form a closely knit group.

1858   Zola leaves Aix for Paris, returning for the holidays with glowing reports of life in the capital. Cézanne is tempted, but remains in Aix. At a second attempt, he gains the baccalauréat. He also continues studies in art at the academy of drawing in Aix begun in 1856.

1859   Studies law at the University of Aix, in compliance with his father's wishes. November, 1859–August, 1860: resumes art training at the academy of drawing.

1861   Abandons law to follow career as artist. In April, goes to Paris at Zola's urging. Meets Pissarro at the Atelier Suisse. But by autumn he is discouraged, returns to Aix and begins work in his father's bank.

1862   Leaves the bank and concentrates once more on painting. Rejoins Zola in Paris where he remains with occasional visits to Aix until 1870.

1863   In Paris probably throughout the year. Exhibits at the notorious Salon des Refusés. Works at the Atelier Suisse, where he meets Guillemet, Oller and Guillaumin.

1864   His works are rejected by the Salon—this is to become a regular occurrence. Copies a painting by Delacroix.

1865   Zola publishes *La Confession de Claude,* dedicated to Cézanne and Baille.

1866   Praised by Zola in the newspaper *L'Événement,* for which Zola is an art critic. His work is again rejected by the Salon. Disgusted, leaves for Aix.

1867–8   Back in Paris. Puts in brief appearances at the Café Guerbois, where Renoir, Manet, Zola and other painters and writers meet.

1870   Works in Aix. On the outbreak of the Franco-Prussian War, to evade service, goes to work at l'Estaque, where he lives secretly with Hortense Fiquet, his mistress.

1871   Returns to Paris in the autumn.

1872   Hortense bears him a son, to whom Cézanne gives his own name, Paul. Goes to Pontoise, where he works with Pissarro, one of whose landscapes he carefully copies.

1873   Begins friendship with Dr. Gachet, one of the first patrons of the Impressionists. Zola publishes *La Ventre de Paris;* one of the characters, Claude Lantier, is based on Cézanne.

1874   At Auvers. Contributes three paintings to the first group exhibition mounted by the Impressionists, whose efforts are ridiculed by both critics and public.

1875   Meets Victor Chocquet, whom he paints (Pls. **14, 17**) and who buys one of his pictures.

1876   In Aix and l'Estaque for the greater part of the year.

1877   Shows sixteen works in the third Impressionist Exhibition. These are not well received, except by the critic Rivière, who anticipates modern reactions in the words: "M. Cézanne is in his work a Greek of the great period; his canvases have the calm and heroic serenity of the paintings and terra-cottas of antiquity. . . ."

1878   In Aix. His father discovers the secret liaison with Hortense Fiquet, but Cézanne refuses to abandon either her or his child.

1879–81	Works at Médan, where Zola has a house; also at Melun, in Paris and at Pontoise.
1880	Meets Huysmans, the art critic and novelist who is then a disciple of Zola.
1881	Is caricatured in a short novel (posthumously published) by Edmond Duranty, an enthusiastic admirer of the Impressionists.
1882	At l'Estaque (with Renoir) and in Paris. Spends five weeks in the autumn with Zola at Médan. Finally gets a portrait exhibited in the Salon.
1883–5	At Aix and l'Estaque. Also visits Paris.
1886	Marries Hortense—with his father and mother as witnesses. Louis-Auguste dies, leaving Cézanne a good income. Zola publishes *L'Oeuvre,* a novel with references that deeply wound Cézanne. The friendship ends.
1887–9	In Aix and in Paris.
1889	Victor Chocquet uses his influence to have Cézanne's *Maison du Pendu* (Pl. 9) shown at the Paris World Fair.
1890	Exhibits three canvases by invitation with *Les XX* in Brussels. Visits Switzerland. Begins to suffer from diabetes.
1891–4	In Aix and in Paris. Visits Monet at Giverny. About 1891, becomes a devout Catholic.
1895	The dealer Vollard organizes Cézanne's first one-man show; the artist contributes 150 paintings. It is from this time that Cézanne's fame dates. Two of his paintings are accepted by the Luxembourg Museum with the Caillebotte bequest.
1896	In Aix. Meets Joachim Gasquet, the first of the young admirers who gather around him in the last years of his life. Zola, in an article, refers to Cézanne as an "abortive genius."

1897–9   Works in Aix, in Paris and Fontainebleau, and at Pontoise. (1897) Two of Cézanne's paintings are hung in the Berlin National Gallery but are banned by the Kaiser. During the Dreyfus Affair, Cézanne disapproves of Zola's stand.

1900   In Aix, the main center of his activities for the rest of his life. Works shown at the Centennial Exhibition in Paris.

1901   Builds a studio on the Chemin des Lauves at Aix. Maurice Denis' *Hommage à Cézanne* shown at the Salon.

1903   Spends the year in Aix. Seven paintings are exhibited at the *Secession* in Vienna, and three in Berlin.

1904   One-man show organized by the Cassirer Gallery in Berlin.

1906   Shows ten paintings at the Salon d'Automne. He is caught in a storm on his way home from a day spent painting out-of-doors; collapses and dies on October 22nd.

LIST OF COLOR PLATES

43. Still-Life. 1882–7.
44. Vase of Flowers. 1883–7.
45. Madame Cézanne. 1883–7.
46. Flowers in a Blue Vase. 1883–7.
47. Vase of Flowers. 1883–7.
48. Nature Morte à la Commode. 1883–7.
49. L'Aqueduc. 1885–7.
50. Arbres et Maisons. 1885–7.
51. Grandes Arbres au Jas de Bouffan. c. 1884.
52. Self-Portrait of the Artist. c. 1884.
53. Portrait of Madame Cézanne. 1885–7.
54. La Montagne Saint-Victoire. 1885–7.
55. The Bather. 1885–7.
56. La Montagne Saint-Victoire. c. 1887.
57. Chestnut Trees at the Jas de Bouffan. c. 1885.
58. Mardi-Gras. 1888.
59. Arlequin. c. 1889(?).
60. Allée à Chantilly. 1888.
61. Aix: Paysage Rocheux. c. 1887.
62. Château de Marines. 1888–90.
63. Still-Life. 1888–90.
64. Madame Cézanne in the Conservatory. c. 1890.
65. The Card Players. 1890–92.
66. Bathing Party. 1892–4.
67. Still-Life. 1890–94.
68. Still-Life with Apples and a Vase of Flowers. 1890–94.
69. La Bouteille de Peppermint. 1890–94.
70. Still-Life. 1890–94.
71. La Maison Lézardée. 1892–4.
72. Portrait of Gustave Geffroy. 1895.
73. Le Garçon au Gilet Rouge. 1894–5.
74. Le Garçon au Gilet Rouge. c. 1894–5.
75. Nature Morte avec l'Amour en Plâtre. c. 1892.
76. Nature Morte avec l'Amour en Plâtre. c. 1892.
77. Le Paysan. 1895–1900.
78. Les Baigneurs. c. 1895.
79. Le Grand Pin. c. 1889.
80. Jeune Italienne Accoudée. c. 1896.
81. Rocky Landscape. 1894–8.
82. La Route Tournante à Montgeroulte. 1898.
83. Still-Life with Apples and Oranges. 1895–1900.
84. Still-Life with Onions and a Bottle. 1895–1900.
85. La Montagne Sainte-Victoire. 1894–1900.
86. Woods with a Millstone. 1898–1900.
87. Bathers. 1900–1906.
88. Le Château Noir. 1904–6.
89. La Montagne Sainte-Victoire. 1904–6.
90. Le Cabanon de Jourdan. 1906.
91. Portrait of Vallier. 1906.
92. Portrait of Vallier (Le Jardinier). c. 1906.

NOTES ON THE COLOR PLATES

1. *Uncle Dominic*. Oil. c. 1866. Collection of Mrs. Ira Haupt, New York. A portrait of Cézanne's uncle, a brother of his mother. Dressing him in a white Dominican robe was no doubt intended as a play on his uncle's name. The use of very thick strokes of paint and the romantic, rather brooding character of the image are evidence of Courbet's influence.

2. *Portrait of Louis-Auguste Cézanne*. Oil. 1868–70. Private Collection, Paris. The artist's father. The coloring is still dark and strong, with strongly accented shadows, and the handling of the paint rather heavy.

3. *The Orgy*. Oil. c. 1866–8. Private Collection, Paris. One of the most avowedly romantic of Cézanne's early paintings, *The Orgy* expresses both the sensuality of his nature and his early love of sensuous art. The style is compounded of elements taken from Veronese and Rubens and Delacroix. Although his style was to develop and change, Cézanne was never to abandon his attempt to create monumental figure compositions (see Pls. 28, 29, 66, 78, and 87), usually with the models nude, as in classical art.

4. *The Picnic*. Oil. c. 1869. Private Collection, Paris. Inspired by Manet's recently exhibited *Dejeuner sur l'herbe* (Louvre), though Cézanne's turbulent imagination and the immaturity of his technique combine to create a less serene effect. The tonality is still fundamentally that of Courbet.

5. *The Black Clock*. Oil. 1869–70. Stavros Niarchos Collection, Paris. This famous picture, which once belonged to Émile Zola, is among the first in which the artist may be said to have found himself. The tonality is still dark, and the textures thick, but there is a decisive attempt now to create a firm composition—evident in the repeated vertical accents formed by the edges and folds of the cloth.

6. *The Man with a Straw Hat.* Oil. 1870–71. Metropolitan Museum of Art, New York. A portrait of Boyer, one of the painter's childhood friends. The texture is very thick, but the paint is manipulated with greater flexibility than in an earlier portrait such as *Uncle Dominic* (Pl. 1).

7. *Melting Snow at l'Estaque.* Oil. 1870–71. E. G. Bührle Collection, Zürich. Painted at L'Estaque, a small port to the west of Marseilles, where Cézanne laid low for six months to avoid military conscription. This is essentially a "landscape of feeling" in the Romantic tradition and in direct contrast to the objective, Impressionist approach that he was shortly to adopt under the influence of Pissarro (see Pl. 9).

8. *A Modern Olympia.* Oil. 1872–3. Louvre, Paris. The theme of this picture, treated by Cézanne in two oils and a watercolor, is an allusion to Manet's *Olympia* (Louvre), which had caused a scandal when shown at the Salon des Refuses in 1863. The present version once belonged to Dr. Paul Gachet, one of the first to appreciate the painter's talents. See Note 11.

9. *La Maison du Pendu (The Suicide's House).* Oil. 1872–3. Louvre, Paris. This is probably the most important work that Cézanne produced in his first year as an Impressionist. In contrast to the earlier paintings (Pls. 1–7), the subject is treated in a straightforward manner; the observation of form and of light is more naturalistic; the composition is steadier; and the paint itself is applied in smaller, less obtrusive strokes. The tonality is much lighter. There is hardly any use of black, shadows being suggested by variations of tone. In all these developments and changes of style the influence of Pissarro is apparent.

10. *Landscape with a House and a Large Tree.* Oil. 1872–3. Collection of Mr. and Mrs. Wm. Goetz, Los Angeles. Impressionist in conception (a landscape by Pissarro even shows the same motif), this work is nevertheless quite personal in its emphatic and rough treatment of paint.

11. *View of Auvers.* Oil. 1874. Art Institute of Chicago. Auvers was a

small village near Paris. The Impressionists often worked there, and received encouragement from Dr. Paul Gachet, a local amateur artist who became a friend and patron of Pissarro and Cézanne and who, some fifteen years later, was to look after Van Gogh. Compared to Pl. 7, this is a much more solidly constructed and straightforwardly conceived landscape.

12. *Fishing*. Oil. 1872–5. Private Collection, Paris. Although in subject-matter this picture harks back to Cézanne's earlier style (Pl. 4), the construction is now more lucid. Note the firm, horizontal emphasis created by the lines of the river bank.

13. *Vase of Flowers*. Oil. 1873–5. Louvre, Paris. Once in Dr. Gachet's collection, this flower-piece was painted at Auvers. Cézanne often took so long over a picture that he was obliged to work from artificial flowers and fruit.

14. *Portrait of Victor Chocquet*. Oil. c. 1875. Collection of Lord Rothschild, Cambridgeshire. Chocquet was a supervisor in the Customs. He was an enthusiastic collector, and after bringing together an excellent collection of works by Delacroix he became interested in the Impressionists and their art. Renoir introduced him to Cézanne in 1875 and they became firm friends. This portrait, which was shown in the third Impressionist Exhibition in 1877, was painted soon after their first meeting.

15. *The Two Vases of Flowers*. Oil. 1873–7. Private Collection, Paris. Cézanne emphasizes the color and structure of the flowers and leaves, but gives little indication of their texture, as a flower painter such as Fantin-Latour would have done.

16. *Madame Cézanne Seated in a Red Armchair*. Oil. c. 1877. Museum of Fine Arts, Boston. Note the frontality of the pose, the solidity of the figure and the reduction of the modelling to a simple statement of the most obvious planes.

17. *Portrait of Victor Chocquet*. Oil. c. 1877. Gallery of Fine Arts, Co-

lumbus, Ohio. This portrait is said to have been painted in the dining room of Chocquet's apartment on the rue de Rivoli. An impression of stability is created by having many of the forms parallel to the picture plane, and their bounding lines parallel to the edges of the painting.

18. *Le Clos des Mathurins à Pontoise*. Oil. 1875–7. Pushkin Museum, Moscow. The same view as painted by Pissarro, but in a less robust and powerfully constructive style.

19. *The Pool at the Jas de Bouffan*. Oil. c. 1878. Private Collection, Paris. The Jas de Bouffan was an estate on the outskirts of Aix that belonged to the Cézanne family until 1899. Various features, notably the avenue of chestnut trees and the ornamental basin shown here, often appear in Cézanne's work. Note the geometrical simplicity, both of the overall design and of the individual forms.

20. *Provençal Landscape*. Water-color. 1875–8. Kunsthaus, Zürich. Cézanne used this medium increasingly in later years, and the pale tonality of water-color influenced his handling of oil paint, as it had in the case of Turner in comparable circumstances.

21. *Bacchanal*. Oil. 1875–6. Collection of Mr. and Mrs. W. Averell Harriman, New York. This painting once belonged to Renoir. The subject is reminiscent of an early work such as *The Orgy* (Pl. 3), but treated in Cézanne's new style.

22. *The Seine at Bercy*. Oil. 1873–5. Kunsthalle, Hamburg. One of Cézanne's most characteristically Impressionist canvases, not only in the composition, but also in the emphasis that is given to human activities. In most of his landscapes, Cézanne entirely ignores human beings.

23. *The Château de Médan*. Water-color. 1879–81. Kunsthaus, Zürich. Émile Zola bought a house at Médan in 1878 and Cézanne visited him there

several times in 1879–82 and in 1885. A magnificent oil painting of this subject, once the property of Gauguin, is now in the Glasgow Art Gallery.

24. *Still-Life with a Fruit-Dish, a Glass and Apples*. Oil. 1877–9. Private Collection, Paris. One of the most celebrated of Cézanne's still-life compositions. It appears in the background of Gauguin's *Portrait of Marie Henry* (Chicago) and is a central feature in Maurice Denis's *Hommage à Cézanne* (Paris, Musée d'Art Moderne).

25. *Still-Life with a Fruit-Dish and Apples*. Oil. 1877–9. Ny Carlsberg Museum, Copenhagen. Closely related in style to the still-life in the preceding plate, with which it also shares its subject matter.

26. *Portrait of Louis Guillaume*. Oil. 1879–82. National Gallery of Art, Washington. Cézanne is the only great artist who has ever excelled equally at landscape, portraiture and still-life. This was possible partly because he reduced all his subject-matter to the status of still-life. His human figures are immobile and their faces are seldom expressive in the conventional sense. He was not interested, like Degas, in conveying the complexities of character.

27. *Self-Portrait*. Oil. c. 1879. National Gallery, London. From the pattern of the wallpaper in the background, it has been deduced that this portrait was painted in Paris, in the apartment at 69 rue de l'Ouest, where Cézanne stayed for a great part of 1877 and at various times in 1879.

28. *Bathers*. Oil. 1879–82. Private Collection, Paris. A clear example of Cézanne's dependence on older art is his figurative compositions: the two prominent bathers are based on figures by Signorelli and Michelangelo.

29. *Three Bathing Women*. Oil. 1879–82. Petit Palais, Paris. This is one of the earlier variants on the theme of "Bathers" which was to occupy Cézanne throughout his life (cf. Pls. 55, 66, 78) and which was to culminate in a series of monumental compositions (Pl. 87, etc.). This canvas once belonged to Henri Matisse, who cherished it and learned much from it.

30. *Landscape in the Île de France.* Oil. 1879–82. Collection of Mr. and Mrs. Wm. Goetz, Los Angeles. A panoramic view, still Impressionistic in its picturesqueness, but already constructive in its execution.

31. *La Route Tournante.* Oil. c. 1881. Museum of Fine Arts, Boston. Painted in the area around Auvers and Pontoise, perhaps between March and December, 1881, when Cézanne was at Pontoise with Pissarro. This is an important example of the artist's maturing powers, a sense of three-dimensional space being reconciled with the surface of the canvas in a far subtler way than he had been capable of in the mid-1870s (cf. Pls. 18 or 19).

32. *Les Peupliers.* Oil. 1879–82. Louvre, Paris. The subtly rendered play of light and shade belies the often-repeated notion that Cézanne was entirely unconcerned with specific effects of luminosity.

33. *La Mer à l'Estaque.* Oil. 1882–5. Private Collection, Paris. Cézanne's preference for solid, tangible forms led him to concentrate on the land; his horizon line is invariably placed high up the canvas, with little room left for the sky, which he often preferred to mask with trees (cf. Pls. 39, 54, 56).

34. *La Montagne Marseillevèyre et l'Île Maire.* Oil. 1882–5. Stirling Collection, Zürich, 1936. The bright red roofs, which Cézanne himself described as playing cards in another painting of this motif, stand out sharply against the surrounding blues and greens.

35. *La Montagne Marseillevèyre.* Water-color. 1882–5. Kunsthaus, Zürich. The same view as Plate 34. Cézanne's water-colors afford an insight into his technique. He would begin with the barest suggestion of form. Completing a picture was a process of constant enrichment.

36. *Le Golfe de Marseille, vu de l'Estaque.* Oil. 1883–5. Louvre, Paris. This picture formed part of the notorious Caillebotte bequest to the Louvre in 1895—"notorious" because the authorities, still suspicious about the Impression-

27

ists, made a great many difficulties about accepting the gift, which included many now acknowledged masterpieces.

37. *Still-Life with Apples, a Bottle and a Soup-Tureen.* Oil. 1883–5. Louvre, Paris. This picture belonged to Pissarro. Cézanne's treatment of perspective was often arbitrary; he would tilt a table—as here—so as to emphasize the flat, two-dimensional character of a design.

38. *Le Pilon du Roi, vue de Bellevue.* Oil. 1884–5. Collection of Mr. and Mrs. Aaron W. Davis. The picture derives its title from the distinctive rock formation silhouetted on the horizon at the right.

39. *View of l'Estaque.* Oil. c. 1885. Butler Collection, London. L'Estaque lies about thirty kilometres to the south of Aix. Cézanne is known to have been working there in 1882, 1883, 1885 and 1889–90.

40. *La Sainte-Victoire, Beaureceuil.* Oil. 1885–6. Herron Art Institute, Indianapolis. Note the great simplicity and angularity of all the forms and the way Cézanne has modified conventional perspective.

41. *View of Gardanne ("Les trois moulins").* Oil. 1885–6. Brooklyn Museum, New York. Though it is obviously unfinished, it is possible that Cézanne completed as much of the painting as he ever intended to. On the other hand, the mid-1880s were a period of great anguish, and he may have cast the canvas aside in a fit of despair.

42. *Le Golfe de Marseille, vue de l'Estaque.* Oil. c. 1886. Art Institute of Chicago. In his landscapes, Cézanne always preferred a detached viewpoint; in his work there is no sense of intimacy with nature, as one finds in the paintings of an artist like Constable. And there are seldom any inhabitants to be found in Cézanne's countryside.

43. *Still-Life.* Oil. 1882–7. Private Collection, Paris. The perspective of

28

this picture is extremely ambiguous. In relation to the table, the floor and wall of the room are much too high. But Cézanne was not interested in the niceties of traditional space-construction. By combining two viewpoints, he was able to give the profusely covered table an appearance of monumentality and stability that would have been lost had it been viewed from above—in accordance with the perspective scheme implied by the background.

44. *Vase of Flowers*. Oil. 1883–7. Private Collection, Paris. A floral arrangement whose coloristic intensity recalls that which is often found in the works of Redon.

45. *Madame Cézanne*. Oil. 1883–7. Collection of Henry P. McIlhenny, Philadelphia. In spite of the insistent simplification of form, the reduction of the face to an almost pure oval, and the emphasis of the stripes, which assume the character of columns in a temple facade, this remains one of the few mature portraits by Cézanne that convey some conventional feeling.

46. *Flowers in a Blue Vase*. Oil. 1883–7. Louvre, Paris. Certain parts of the picture, notably the two apples in the lower right hand corner, are less highly finished, in accordance with the artist's principle that there were certain areas in a design that needed fuller and richer treatment than the subsidiary parts.

47. *Vase of Flowers*. Oil. 1883–7. Private Collection, Paris. Note how the background is reduced to what is virtually a geometric pattern—a process that already foreshadows the abstraction of Mondrian. Note also the virtual elimination of cast shadows.

48. *Nature Morte à la Commode*. Oil. 1883–7. Fogg Art Museum, Cambridge, Mass. Although Cézanne came to distrust imaginative compositions, always preferring to work from the motif, he was by no means averse to a manipulation of his subject matter, as is evident in the Baroque swirl of drapery here.

49. *L'Aqueduc*. Oil. 1885–7. Pushkin Museum, Moscow. Although the

forms in Cézanne's mature paintings are more or less static, there are occasional passages, such as the vortex of branches in the present picture, which seem to hint at passion and violence that he was at pains to avoid in his work.

50. *Arbres et Maisons*. Oil. 1885–7. Private Collection, Paris. A landscape interesting for its motif: the distinct view framed by a screen of trees in the foreground, whose branches form an elaborate arabesque.

51. *Grandes Arbres au Jas de Bouffan*. Oil. c. 1884. Private Collection, Pennsylvania. The picture represents trees by the garden wall on the west side of the Jas de Bouffan. The subject was also treated in a horizontal picture, now in the Courtauld Gallery, London.

52. *Self-Portrait of the Artist*. Oil. c. 1884. E. G. Bührle Foundation, Zürich. The conception of this picture is curious: Cézanne is obviously in a room, and yet the background suggests the open sky. The composition was perhaps suggested by Rembrandt's late *Self-Portrait* in the Louvre.

53. *Portrait of Madame Cézanne*. Oil. 1885–7. Private Collection, Paris. In comparison with Plate 45, a more impersonal portrait, yet the inclination of the head still suggests a sad perverseness.

54. *La Montagne Sainte-Victoire*. Oil. 1885–7. Metropolitan Museum of Art, New York. The Montagne Sainte-Victoire became Cézanne's favorite motif in the last twenty years or so of his life. He painted it from various angles. This version was painted from Bellevue, to the south of Aix, where his brother-in-law had bought an estate in 1885.

55. *The Bather*. Oil. 1885–7. Museum of Modern Art, New York. Although the treatment was modern, the theme of The Bather was highly traditional and emphasizes Cézanne's respects for the art of the past.

56. *La Montagne Sainte-Victoire*. Oil. c. 1887. Courtauld Gallery, London.

Note how the sense of distance is contrasted and yet also reconciled with a sense of two-dimensional pattern that covers the whole canvas. The branches in particular fulfill a decorative, rhythmic function in the design, as well as blotting out an unwanted expanse of empty sky.

57. *Chestnut Trees at the Jas de Bouffan*. Oil. c. 1885. Institute of Arts, Minneapolis. The family house, built in the 17th century, is on the left; the mountain in the distance is the Sainte-Victoire (cf. Pls. 54 and 56).

58. *Mardi-Gras*. Oil. 1888. Pushkin Museum, Moscow. One of the very few anecdotal pictures of Cézanne's maturity, the *Mardi-Gras* was painted in Paris. Comparisons with Watteau or Daumier emphasize the lack of what might be termed dramatic interest. The poetry of the painting stems not from its mood or range of emotional observation, but from the delicacy with which the forms are constructed.

59. *Arlequin*. Oil. c. 1889(?). Collection of Lord Rothschild, Cambridgeshire. This is likely to have been a development from, and not a preparatory study for the *Mardi-Gras* (Pl. 58). The treatment of the head in particular is more summary and abstract.

60. *Allée à Chantilly*. Oil. 1888. Collection of William A. M. Burden, Washington, D.C. An intriguing view of the famous chateau, which seems formally framed, yet is oddly cut by the trees and impossible to complete mentally.

61. *Aix: Paysage Rocheux*. Oil. c. 1887. National Gallery, London. A fine example of Cézanne's complex art. Firmness and stability of design are combined with a vivid sense of space and distance, even of sunlight, and the structure of the rocks is suggested with extraordinary economy and force—and all this without any pretense that the paint strokes are anything but tiny dabs of variously colored pigment!

62. *Château de Marines*. Oil. 1888–90. Collection of Mr. and Mrs. J. K.

Thannhauser, New York. This picture provides a good example of the way Cézanne manipulated space for pictorial reasons. The chateau in the center of the painting is actually much further back than the house on the left, but *looks* as if it were a tiny building on the same plane.

63. *Still-Life*. Oil. 1888–90. National Gallery, Oslo. The ambiguous perspective creates the impression that the table surface is upright and parallel with the picture plane. This device both foreshadowed and influenced the development of Synthetic Cubism (compare still-lifes by Braque and Picasso).

64. *Madame Cézanne in the Conservatory*. Oil. c. 1890. Metropolitan Museum of Art, New York. This is an unfinished picture, yet one that is tender and spring-like in feeling.

65. *The Card Players*. Oil. 1890–92. Louvre, Paris. Cézanne painted five versions of this theme. Two of them have three players and spectators, and three of them only two players. The models were peasants and day-laborers at the Jas de Bouffan. All the variants are devoid of the kind of drama with which artists like Caravaggio had invested the subject in the 17th century. The larger and more elaborate versions suggest that in the composition Cézanne may have been influenced by pictures of the *Supper at Emmaus,* such as those of Titian and Rembrandt in the Louvre.

66. *Bathing Party*. Oil. 1892–4. Private Collection, Paris. In comparison with earlier versions (cf. Pls. 28, 29), this composition is more "architectural"; the human bodies are now given a greater emphasis and stand out more clearly from the background.

67. *Still-Life*. Oil. 1890–94. Private Collection, New York. One of the exemplary Cézanne still-lifes, in which a pile of apples assumes a monumental massiveness and weight.

68. *Still-Life with Apples and a Vase of Flowers*. Oil. 1890–94. Art Insti-

tute of Chicago. A more delicately poetic conception than in the preceding still-life, and painted in lighter, clearer colors.

69. *La Bouteille de Peppermint*. Oil. 1890–94. National Gallery of Art, Washington. The curves and scroll-patterns in the blue tablecloth introduce a powerful element of movement into this representation of inanimate objects.

70. *Still-Life*. Oil. 1890–94. Art Institute of Chicago. Cézanne took so long over his paintings that he often had to resort to painting wax fruit and flowers. They were not as natural, but at least they did not wilt or go bad.

71. *La Maison Lézardée*. Oil. 1892–4. Collection of Mrs. Ira Haupt, New York. A romantic vision of an abandoned house in ruins, recalling Poe's famous story, "The Fall of the House of Usher."

72. *Portrait of Gustave Geffroy*. Oil. 1895. Private Collection, Paris. Geffroy was a novelist and art critic, and a great champion of the Impressionists. This portrait of his is among the finest and most elaborate of all Cézanne's works: the figure, a triangular form on the surface, dominates, but never overpowers the composition. There is great austerity, but it does not preclude richness of detail, or an extraordinary delicacy in the coloring and the handling.

73. *Le Garçon au Gilet Rouge*. Oil. 1894–5. E. G. Bührle Foundation, Zürich. The sitter was a young Italian, apparently named Michelangelo di Rosa; Cézanne made one water-color and three other oil paintings of him (cf. Pl. 74).

74. *Le Garçon au Gilet Rouge*. Oil. c. 1894–5. Rockefeller Collection, New York. See Note 73. This portrait was painted in Geffroy's library. Cézanne despaired of ever finishing it.

75. *Nature Morte avec l'Amour en Plâtre*. Oil. c. 1892. Courtauld Gallery, London. The central feature is a plaster cast after a Cupid then attributed to Puget. The cast is now preserved—though headless—in the studio at Aix. At

the left is a picture, propped up against the wall, and showing fruit on a blue cloth—the same kind of blue cloth, in fact, as lies on the table next to the Cupid.

76. *Nature Morte avec l'Amour en Plâtre*. Oil. c. 1892. National Museum, Stockholm. The same objects as in the still-life in Plate 75, but less radically distorted, and rendered in a looser, more flickering technique.

77. *Le Paysan*. Oil. 1895–1900. Ex-Conger-Goodyear Collection, New York. For many of his later figure pieces, which required a great many sittings, Cézanne would often use professional models (when in Paris), or servants and local laborers (when in Aix).

78. *Les Baigneurs*. Oil. c. 1895. Baltimore, Museum of Art. A wide, frieze-like composition in which motives both from earlier bather pictures (see Pls. 28, 68) and the earlier *Lutte d'Amour* (see Pl. 21) are combined.

79. *Le Grand Pin*. Oil. c. 1889. Museum of Art, São Paulo, Brazil. This study was made at Montbriant. The imagery is unusually forceful for Cézanne at this date, and brings to mind a poem he had written in 1863:

> "The tree shaken by the fury of the winds,
>   Stirs in the air its stripped branches,
>   Like an immense cadaver that the mistral swings."

80. *Jeune Italienne Accoudée*. Oil. c. 1896. Collection of Dr. and Mrs. Harry Bakwin, New York. The model is said to have been the daughter of an Italian who posed for the artist in 1893, and closely related to the boy in the red waistcoat (cf Pls. 73 and 74). The pose, with the head resting on one hand, was used by Cézanne on several occasions (cf. Pl. 73).

81. *Rocky Landscape*. Oil. 1894–8. Metropolitan Museum of Art, New York. The scene probably represents a section of the forest at Fontainebleau, which had been popular with Corot and the Barbizon painters.

82. *La Route Tournante à Montgeroult.* Oil. 1898. Collection of John Hay Whitney, New York. This is among the last important works to be painted by Cézanne in Northern France. Montgeroult is a village near Pontoise; the artist stayed there during the summer of 1898. This is a good example of Cézanne's mature style, with its extreme simplifications of form suggested by a framework of exposed brush-strokes.

83. *Still-Life with Apples and Oranges.* Oil. 1895–1900. Louvre, Paris. One of the most richly colored and sensuous of Cézanne's later still-lifes, in which his passionate temperament temporarily gains the upper hand.

84. *Still-Life with Onions and a Bottle.* Oil. 1895–1900. Louvre, Paris. An extraordinarily subtle and delicate picture in which there are also elements of great force, such as the cascading drapery at the right.

85. *La Montagne Sainte-Victoire.* Oil. 1894–1900. Pushkin Museum, Moscow. See Note 54.

86. *Woods with a Millstone.* Oil. 1898–1900. Collection of Carrol S. Tyson, Philadelphia. An example of Cézanne's work in which not only the construction but also the subject has a geometrical emphasis. It is but a short step to early Cubism. And yet for all its apparent artificiality, photographs of the site, which was in the neighbourhood of the Château Noir, show how faithful Cézanne was to the motif.

87. *Bathers.* Oil. 1900–1906. Philadelphia Museum of Art. This is the largest of all of Cézanne's compositions of nude figures. Another version is now in the National Gallery, London. These pictures caused the artist an immense amount of trouble and he worked on them for years. At his death they were still more or less unfinished. The architectonic character is particularly clear in this version. The inclined trunks of the trees are like the piers of a cathedral arch.

88. *Le Château Noir.* Oil. 1904–6. Collection of Dr. and Mrs. David M.

Levy, New York. Cézanne's handling became increasingly free in his very late works, of which this is a typical example; it foreshadows a form of pure abstraction.

89. *La Montagne Sainte-Victoire*. Oil. 1904–6. Collection of Carrol S. Tyson, Philadelphia. See Notes 85 and 88.

90. *Le Cabanon de Jourdan*. Oil. 1906. Oeffentliche Kunstsammlungen, Basle. This is the picture on which Cézanne was working just before he died, thus fulfilling his earlier vow to die while painting.

91. *Portrait of Vallier*. Oil. 1906. Collection of Mr. and Mrs. Leigh B. Block, Chicago. Vallier was Cézanne's gardener and odd-job man at the Chemin des Lauves, where the artist had built a studio in 1901. He was working on this picture in the weeks before his death. The technique has all the delicacy of water-color.

92. *Portrait of Vallier (Le Jardinier)*. Oil. c. 1906. Tate Gallery, London. Painted in the garden outside the studio at the Chemin des Lauves.

THE PLATES

1 *Uncle Dominic.* Oil. 25⅝ × 21¼ in. c. 1866. Collection of Mrs. Ira Haupt, New York.
Brooding, powerful, yet technically inept, this is typical of Cézanne's earliest work.

2 *Portrait of Louis-Auguste Cézanne.*   Oil.   80 × 48 in.   **1868–70.**   Private Collection, Paris.
Cézanne reduces the human being to the status of still-life even in this early picture.

3 *The Orgy*. Oil. 51 ° × 31⅞ in. c. 1866–8. Private Collection, Paris. Indicative of Cézanne's passionate temperament and respect for Delacroix and the Venetians.

4 *The Picnic*.   Oil.   23⅝ × 31⅞ in.   c. 1869.   Private Collection, Paris.   Strength of feeling
and lack of facility give a gentle theme sinister overtones.

5 *The Black Clock*.　　Oil.　　21¾ × 29¼ in.　　**1869–70**.　　Stavros Niarchos Collection, Paris.
The stability of the composition is an advance over the preceding examples.

6 *The Man with a Straw Hat.* Oil. 21⅝ × 15⅜ in. 1870–71. Metropolitan Museum of Art, New York. Among the most accomplished of Cézanne's early "romantic" works.

7 *Melting Snow at l'Estaque.* Oil. 28¾ × 36¼ in. 1870–71. E. G. Bührle Collection, Zürich. Cézanne is now paying more attention to direct observation of everyday phenomena.

8 *A Modern Olympia.*   Oil.   18⅛ × 21⅞ in.   1872–3.   Louvre, Paris.   A parody of Manet that is also a highly personal erotic daydream.

9 *La Maison du Pendu* (*The Suicide's House*).   Oil.   20⅜ × 26⅝ in.   1872–3.   Louvre, Paris.
Cézanne is now under the influence of the Impressionist Camille Pissarro.

10 *Landscape with a House and a Large Tree.*   Oil.   26⅝ × 22 in.   1872–3.   Coll.: Mr. and Mrs. Wm. Goetz, L.A.   The forms are depicted as they appear in sunlight—an Impressionist concern.

11 *View of Auvers*. Oil. 25½ × 31½ in. 1874. Art Institute of Chicago. A panoramic view of the village near Paris that was popular with the Impressionists.

12 *Fishing*.   Oil.   10⅞ × 14⅞ in.   1872–5.   Private Collection, Paris.   A traditional subject, which Cézanne has stripped of its narrative associations.

13 *Vase of Flowers*.   Oil.   16¼ × 10¾ in.   1873–5.   Louvre, Paris.   A slow worker, Cézanne found still-life (often artificial fruits or flowers) a convenient subject-matter.

14 *Portrait of Victor Chocquet.* Oil. 18 × 14½ in. c. **1875.** Collection of Lord Rothschild, Cambridgeshire. Chocquet was one of the first to appreciate the artist's work.

15 *The Two Vases of Flowers.* Oil. 22× 17⅝ in. 1873–7. Private Collection, Paris. Cézanne emphasizes the individual colors but not the textures of the flowers.

16   *Madame Cézanne Seated in a Red Armchair.*   Oil.   29 × 22½ in.   c. 1877.   Museum of Fine Arts, Boston.   This informal portrait makes an extraordinarily monumental impression.

17 *Portrait of Victor Chocquet*. Oil. 18 × 15 in. c. 1877. Gallery of Fine Arts, Columbus, Ohio. The brush-strokes themselves contribute to the painting's geometrical character.

18 *Le Clos des Mathurins à Pontoise*.   Oil.   23¼ × 28½ in.   1875–7.   Pushkin Museum, Moscow.   The perspective is treated in the manner of Pissarro, who painted the same view.

19 *The Pool at the Jas de Bouffan.* Oil. 21 × 22⅜ in. c. 1878. Private Collection, Paris.
The ornamental basin in the gardens of the "Jas de Bouffan," the family home near Aix.

20 *Provençal Landscape.* Water-color. 1875–8. Kunsthaus, Zürich. The delicacy of Cézanne's perceptions is particular evident in water-colors such as this one.

21 *Bacchanal.* Oil. 15 × 18⅛ in. 1875–6. Coll.: Mr. and Mrs. W. Averell Harriman, New York. A theme of Venetian Renaissance art, but treated not as an idyll so much as struggle.

22 *The Seine at Bercy.* Oil. 24 × 29 in. 1873–5. Kunsthalle, Hamburg. Human activity is rarely depicted by Cézanne in his landscapes.

23 *The Château de Médan*. Water-color. 12⅜ × 18⅞ in. 1879–81. Kunsthaus, Zürich. The emphatic verticals and horizontals contribute to the stability of the composition.

24 *Still-Life with a Fruit-Dish, a Glass and Apples.* Oil. 18⅛ × 21⅝ in. 1877–9. Private Collection, Paris. One of the first of Cézanne's mature masterpieces.

25 *Still-Life with a Fruit-Dish and Apples.* Oil. 17 × 21⅝ in. **1877–9.** Ny Carlsberg Museum, Copenhagen. Cézanne often repeated his compositions with only slight variations (cf. Pl. 24).

26 *Portrait of Louis Guillaume.*   Oil.   22 × 18½ in.   1879–82.   National Gallery of Art, Washington.   The face is reduced almost to a mask, yet still seems moving and true.

27 *Self-Portrait*. Oil. 14½ × 11½ in. c. 1879. National Gallery, London. Cézanne, like Van Gogh and Rembrandt, was a prolific self-portraitist.

28 *Bathers.* Oil. 7½ × 10⅜ in. 1879–82. Private Collection, Paris. A traditional theme chosen for its formal, structural possibilities rather than for its poetry.

29 *Three Bathing Women*. Oil. **17** × **19½** in. 1879–82. Petit Palais, Paris. Figures of this kind influenced the *Nu de dos* relief sculpture of Matisse, who owned this painting.

30 *Landscape in the Île de France*.   Oil.   24 × 29¼ in.   1879–82.   Coll.: Mr. and Mrs. Wm.
Goetz, Los Angeles.   Cézanne was always fond of panoramas that inspired feelings of exaltation.

31 *La Route Tournante*.   Oil.   23½ × 28¾ in.   c. 1881.   Museum of Fine Arts, Boston.   An important example of Cézanne's maturing powers in construction and coloring.

32 *Les Peupliers*.   Oil.   24⅞ × 31¼ in.   1879–82.   Louvre, Paris.   Like many Impressionists, Cézanne painted scenery of no intrinsic beauty or importance.

33 *La Mer à l'Estaque.* Oil. 26 × 32⅜ in. 1882–5. Private Collection, Paris. Trees are used to frame the scene and blot out unwanted sky.

34 *La Montagne Marseillevèyre et l'Île Marie.*   Oil.   20¼ × 24 in.   1882–5.   Stirling Collection, Zürich, 1936.   The red roofs become strongly defined points of visual emphasis.

35 *La Montagne Marseillevèyre.*   Water-color.   11¼ × 18⅛ in.   1882–5.   Kunsthaus, Zürich.
In his mature period water-color and oils become for Cézanne interchangeable media.

36 *Le Golfe de Marseille, vu de l'Estaque.* Oil. 23¼ × 28¾ in. 1883–5. Louvre, Paris. The Mediterranean coast-line was one of Cézanne's favorite subjects.

37 *Still-Life with Apples, a Bottle and a Soup-Tureen.* Oil. 26 × 32⅝ in. 1883–5. Louvre, Paris. The effect is monumental, yet the design simple and the subject matter humble.

38 *Le Pilon du Roi, vue de Bellevue.* Oil. 21½ × 25½ in. 1884–5. Private Collection. The basic common denominator here is the small, squarish brush-stroke.

39 *View of l'Estaque*. Oil. 28 × 22¾ in. c. 1885. Butler Collection, London. The grandeur and balance of the composition recall such 17th-century painters as Poussin and Claude.

40 *La Sainte-Victoire, Beaureceuil.* Oil. 25⅝ × 31⅞ in. 1885–6. Herron Art Institute, Indianapolis. The reticence of Cézanne's style was ideally suited to bare, stony landscape.

41 *View of Gardanne ("Les trois moulins").* Oil. 35¼ × 28¾ in. 1885–6. Brooklyn Museum, New York. Painted in a period of great emotional stress, this is nevertheless serene.

42 *Le Golfe de Marseille, vue de l'Estaque.* Oil. 29⅞ × 38¼ in. c. 1886. Art Institute of Chicago. The high viewpoint is common in Cézanne's work and provides a panoramic vista.

43 *Still-Life*. Oil. 24 × 29¼ in. 1882–7. Private Collection, Paris. The objects in Cézanne's still-lifes were usually studio bric-a-brac or are taken from the kitchen.

44 *Vase of Flowers*. Oil. 27¼ × 22¾ in. 1883–7. Private Collection, Paris. The plainness of the background throws the flowers into greater relief.

45 *Madame Cézanne.* Oil. 24⅜ × 20⅛ in. 1883–7. Collection of Henry P. McIlhenny, Philadelphia. There is here an intensity of feeling that is otherwise rare in Cézanne's work.

46 *Flowers in a Blue Vase.* Oil. 24⅜ × 20 in. 1883–7. Louvre, Paris. The carefully contrived asymmetry is a characteristically Impressionist device.

47 *Vase of Flowers.* Oil. 21¾ × 18¼ in. 1883–7. Private Collection, Paris. In Cézanne's mature work the shadows are light and pale, as in the table here.

48 *Nature Morte à la Commode.* Oil. 25⅝ × 31⅞ in. 1883–7. Fogg Art Museum, Cambridge, Mass. The tablecloth is given the unyielding character of stone.

49 *L'Aqueduc.* Oil. 36¾ × 29¼ in. 1885–7. Pushkin Museum, Moscow. In the distance is a Roman viaduct which Cézanne often depicted in his views of the Arc valley.

50 *Arbres et Maisons*. Oil. 27¼ × 36¾ in. 1885–7. Private Collection, Paris. Like other Impressionists, Cézanne favored a high color key.

51 *Grands Arbres au Jas de Bouffan.* Oil. 27⅝ × 23¼ in. c. 1884. Private Collection, Pennsylvania. The effect of dappled sunlight is caught here brilliantly.

52 *Self-Portrait of the Artist.* Oil. 36¼ × 28¾ in. c. **1884.** E. G. Bührle Collection, Zürich. The composition recalls in some respects the late Rembrandt self-portrait in the Louvre.

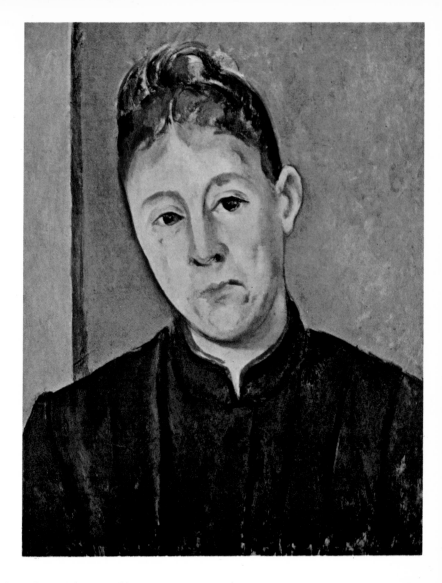

53 *Portrait of Madame Cézanne.* Oil. 18½ × 15¼ in. 1885–7. Private Collection, Paris. The features are greatly simplified, yet the personality and mood are captured.

54　*La Montagne Sainte-Victoire.* Oil.　25⅝ × 31⅞ in.　**1885–7.**　Metropolitan Museum of Art, New York.　Distance is implied but the sense of space is not stressed.

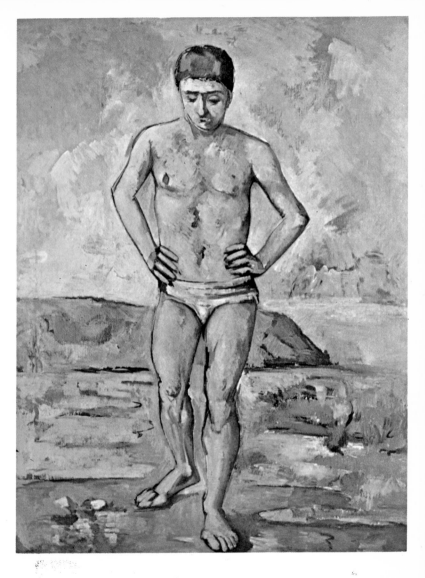

55 *The Bather*. Oil. 50 × 38⅛ in. 1885–7. Museum of Modern Art, New York. A traditional theme, treated in a modern way, and especially remarkable for its vigorous execution.

56 *La Montagne Sainte-Victoire.* Oil. 26 × 35½ in. c. 1887. Courtauld Gallery, London. The undulating branches introduce an almost Oriental rhythm into the design.

57 *Chestnut Trees at the Jas de Bouffan.* Oil. 28¾ × 36½ in. c. 1885. Institute of Arts, Minneapolis. One of Cézanne's simplest, yet most stately and effective designs.

58 *Mardi Gras*. Oil. 40× 32⅝ in. 1888. Pushkin Museum, Moscow. One of the artist's rare anecdotal pictures, foreshadowing in its circus theme Picasso's early work.

59 *Arlequin*. Oil. 36¼ × 25½ in. c. 1889?. Collection of Lord Rothschild, Cambridgeshire. Cézanne often made careful studies for important paintings, such as this one for Pl. 58.

60 *Allée à Chantilly.* Oil. 31⅞ × 25⅝ in. 1888. Coll.: W. A. M. Burden, Washington, D.C.
The huge trees seem to dwarf the famous chateau, but its distance is hard to determine.

61 *Aix: Paysage Rocheux.* Oil. 25½ × 32 in. c. 1887. National Gallery, London. Sunlight, space and physical structure are all suggested in this seemingly simple painting.

62 *Château de Marines*. Oil. 29½ × 36¼ in. 1888–90. Coll.: Mr. and Mrs. J. K. Thannhauser, New York. Cézanne's use of color, particularly blue and green, was always extremely delicate.

63 *Still-Life*. Oil. 23¾ × 29 in. 1888–90. National Gallery, Oslo. Cézanne's often inconsistent perspective is seen in the oddly tilted table and floor planes.

64 *Madame Cézanne in the Conservatory.* Oil. 36½ × 28½ in. c. 1890. Metropolitan Museum of Art, New York. The design, with the figure forming a triangle, is of classic simplicity.

65 *The Card Players.* Oil. 18 × 22⅞ in. 1890–92. Louvre, Paris. Cézanne painted the subject of card-players five times in the early 1890s.

66 *Bathing Party*. Oil. 24 × 32⅜ in. 1892–4. Private Collection, Paris. Monumental treatment of the bodies invests a casual theme with the grandeur of Renaissance art.

67 *Still-Life*.   Oil.   18½ × 21⅝ in.   1890–94.   Private Collection, New York.   All the forms have great geometric simplicity, yet are subtly distorted and thus complex.

68 *Still-Life with Apples and a Vase of Flowers.* Oil. 23¼ × 16⅞ in. 1890–94. Art Institute of Chicago. The table is seen from above, the flowers from the side.

69 *La Bouteille de Peppermint*. Oil. 25⅞ × 32¼ in. 1890–94. National Gallery of Art, Washington. The curves in the cloth introduce a curious sense of motion.

70 *Still-Life*. Oil. 24⅜ × 31 in. 1890–94. Art Institute of Chicago. Cézanne's still-lifes are always an arrangement for painting, never a breakfast table or loaded side-board.

71 *La Maison Lézardée*. Oil. 26 × 21⅝ in. 1892–4. Collection of Mrs. Ira Haupt, New York.
A dramatic work, akin in mood to the pictures of Van Gogh.

72 *Portrait of Gustave Geffroy.* Oil. 46¼ × 36 in. 1895. Private Collection, Paris. An elaborate portrait of a well known critic and novelist of the day.

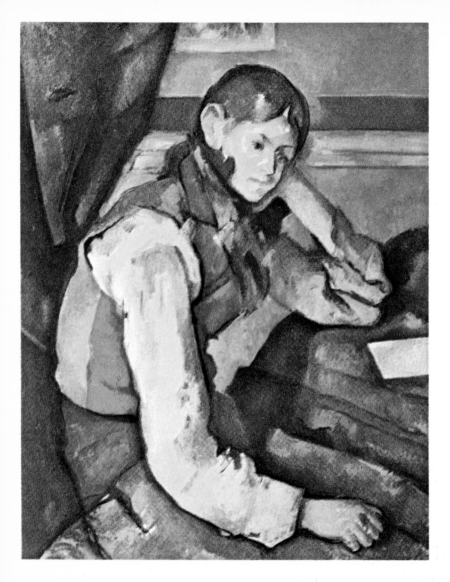

73 *Le Garçon au Gilet Rouge.* Oil. 31¼ × 25⅛ in. 1894–5. E. G. Bührle Collection, Zürich. The model was a young Italian, apparently named Michelangelo di Rosa.

74 *Le Garçon au Gilet Rouge.* Oil. 36½ × 28¾ in. c. **1894–5**. Rockefeller Collection, New York.
This picture gave the artist a great deal of trouble, yet is thinly painted in places.

75 *Nature Morte avec l'Amour en Plâtre*. Oil. 27½ × 22½ in. c. 1892. Courtauld Gallery, London. One of Cézanne's most spatially complex and even ambivalent works.

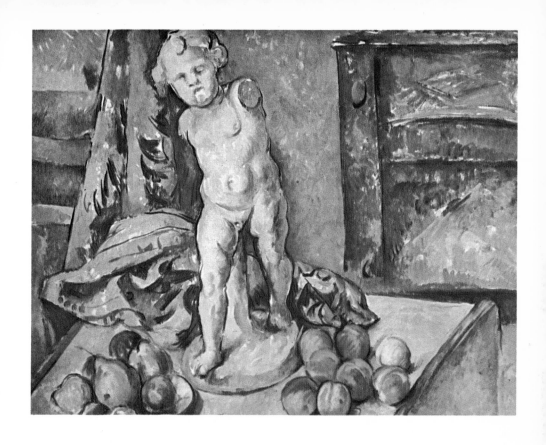

76 *Nature Morte avec l'Amour en Plâtre*.   Oil.   25¼ × 32¼ in.   c. 1892.   National Museum, Stockholm.   The central feature is a plaster cast after a *Cupid* then attributed to Puget.

77 *Le Paysan.* Oil. 32 × 26 in. 1895–1900. Ex-Conger-Goodyear Collection, New York. The models for many of the late works were peasants and laborers.

78 *Les Baigneurs*. Oil. 10⅕ × 18⅖ in. c. 1895. Baltimore Museum of Art. The classical theme of Bathers preoccupied Cézanne throughout his life.

79　*Le Grand Pin*.　Oil.　33½ × 36¼ in.　c. 1889.　Museum of Art, São Paulo, Brazil.　One of the most romantic of Cézanne's mature landscapes.

80 *Jeune Italienne Accoudée.* Oil. 36¼ × 28¾ in. c. 1896. Collection of Dr. and Mrs. Harry Bakwin, New York. The composition is similar to that in Pl. **73**, but in reverse.

81 *Rocky Landscape*. Oil. 29¼ × 36⅞ in. 1894–8. Metropolitan Museum of Art, New York.
Cézanne could make a fine picture out of the most unpromising material.

82 *La Route Tournante à Montgeroult*. Oil. 32 × 25⅝ in. 1898. Coll.: John Hay Whitney, New York. The brush-strokes are obviously just that, tiny loads of pigment side by side.

83 *Still-Life with Apples and Oranges.* Oil. 29¼ × 36⅞ in. 1895–1900. Louvre, Paris. Among the richest and most sensuous of the late still-lifes.

84 *Still-Life with Onions and a Bottle.* Oil. 26½ × 32½ in. 1895–1900. Louvre, Paris. Cézanne invests the draped cloth with the majestic force of a cataract.

85 *La Montagne Sainte-Victoire*. Oil. 26 × 32½ in. 1894–1900. Pushkin Museum, Moscow. This
mountain near Aix-en-Provence was Cézanne's favorite motif in the period 1880–1906.

86   *Woods with a Millstone.*   Oil.   29½ × 36¾ in.   1898–1900.   Collection of Carrol S. Tyson, Philadelphia.   From a painting like this it is but a short step to Cubism.

87 *Bathers*. Oil. 82 × 98 in. 1900–1906. Philadelphia Museum of Art. The largest and grandest of the paintings of Bathers, on which Cézanne worked for about a decade.

88 *Le Château Noir.* Oil. 29¼ × 36¾ in. 1904–6. Coll.: Dr. and Mrs. David M. Levy, New
York. Many of the late works, though based on careful observation, are almost abstract.

89 *La Montagne Sainte-Victoire*. Oil. 25⅝ × 31⅞ in. 1904–6. Coll.: Carrol S. Tyson, Phila-delphia. Trees, rocks, roads—all forms are magnificently described in a summary manner.

90 *Le Cabanon de Jourdan*. Oil. 26 × 32½ in. 1906. Collection of Mr. and Mrs. Leigh B. Block, Chicago. Cézanne's last painting, the one he was working on when taken ill.

91 *Portrait of Vallier*. Oil. 25½ × 21¼ in. 1906. Collection of Mr. and Mrs. Leigh B. Block, Chicago. A portrait of Cézanne's gardener and odd-job man, invested with a noble grandeur.

92 *Portrait of Vallier* (*Le Jardinier*). Oil. 25 × 21 in. c. 1906. Tate Gallery, London. Almost a composite in which portrait, landscape and still-life seem inextricably blended.